IMAGES
of America

DEEP SOUTH
AVIATION

The F-4 Phantom's nose points to the front of the Southern Museum of Flight. The two homebuilts shown inside are Les Holland's Piel Emeraude on the left, and a BD-4 on the right. (Courtesy of Bob Kendrick.)

IMAGES
of America

DEEP SOUTH
AVIATION

Dr. Don Dodd
and Dr. Amy Bartlett-Dodd

ARCADIA
PUBLISHING

Published by Arcadia Publishing
Charleston, South Carolina

Library of Congress Catalog Card Number: Applied for

For all general information contact Arcadia Publishing at:
Telephone 843-853-2070
Fax 843-853-0044
E-Mail sales@arcadiapublishing.com
For customer service and orders:
Toll-Free 1-888-313-2665

Visit us on the Internet at www.arcadiapublishing.com

This image of Orville and Wilbur Wright's 1903 flight at Kill Devil Hill, Kitty Hawk, North Carolina, was made from the original glass negative. Wilkerson Wright, a descendant of the Wright brothers, gave the photo to the Southern Museum of Flight.

CONTENTS

An early "Flying Machine" was built by John Fowler of Mobile soon after the Wright Brothers 1903 flight. (SMF photo.)

ACKNOWLEDGMENTS

Specific credits for photographs used are given at the end of each caption. The Southern Museum of Flight (SMF) photo credit is a broad umbrella that covers hundreds of museum contributors from the first collections of Mary Alice Beatty at Samford University in the 1960s to the last DOG (donor of gift) signed by Collections Manager Wade Meyers. As Joe Shannon once said, "*You* know who you are."

A special thanks is extended to Dr. J. Dudley Pewitt, Chairman of the Board and Executive Director, members of the museum board who have encouraged the project from the start, and to all the supporters of the museum through the years who have made it a place where such a book could be produced.

The museum staff were all helpful—Glenda McCarroll and Pat Williams up front, Deborah Stone and Wade upstairs, Ira Jackson out back, and Mike Callahan everywhere. We will always remember Cecil Greene going through his storage areas to find excellent photos of the National Guard, Richard Reeve taking a half-day from a busy schedule to supply needed shots, J.J. and Tom Bartlett contributing a day of work at a critical time, Joe Shannon passing on needed materials in a late-night rendezvous, Alvin Hudson making two special trips to reproduce items from his collection, and Curtis Anthony and Bruce Gragg at Wolf Camera for timely photographic advice on several occasions.

Additionally, Joe Caver of USAFHRA was particularly helpful with Tuskegee Airmen materials, and Archie DiFante of the same shop on different topics. Most of all we appreciate the consideration, thoughtfulness, and good nature of our daughter, Lorene, who made the project go ever so much smoother on the home front.

INTRODUCTION

Birmingham has long been a center of aviation in the Deep South, which is well documented in the holdings of the Southern Museum of Flight (SMF) near the Birmingham International Airport. Airplanes have been built or repaired here—from Glenn Messer's "Air Boss" of the 1920s–1930s through Bechtel-McCone of World War II, Hayes Aircraft, and now Pemco. The Air Squadron of the Alabama National Guard was founded in Birmingham by World War I flyers and its history is chronicled in SMF display cases and photographic wall displays. A planned exhibit on the Bay of Pigs (including a T-33 jet and B-26 Douglas Invader) honors the four Birmingham Guardsmen killed in the April 1961 action. The F-4 Phantom jet in front of the Museum accents the Guard's use of that versatile aircraft of the Vietnam era. The Birmingham airfields wall display illustrates early aviation at Dixie Field, Messer Field, Roberts Field, and the Birmingham Municipal Airport (now the Birmingham International Airport). Fifty-five plaques and biographical sketches in the Alabama Aviation Hall of Fame pay homage to Deep South aviation pioneers who made air travel a way of life. Frank Hulse's Southern Airways was headquartered at Birmingham Municipal Airport, and Delta had initial routes through Birmingham. Favorable flying weather contributed to numerous military airfields in the South. Deep South flying fields will be featured in a Museum trainer exhibit which now includes the basic (BT-13 Vultee Valiant), primary (PT 19 Fairchild Cornell), and advanced (AT-6 Texan) trainers of the World War II era and the T-33 jet of the post-war era.

Thus, in the fields of aircraft construction and repair, Air Guard activity, early airfields, aviation leadership, airline evolution, and military training bases, Birmingham has been a center of Alabama and Deep South aviation history from the 1920s to the present. *Deep South Aviation* cuts across all of these themes but in a selective way as it is limited to historic photographs available in the museum or from friends of the museum. The coverage is further delimited by the need for reasonably sharp black-and-white images complicated by the frequent requirement to "photograph photographs." At least half of the accumulated photographs were eliminated due to poor quality.

With these constraints, a comprehensive, in-depth compilation was obviously impossible. An attempt was made to produce adequate reproductions from each topical theme of the museum's holdings. Examples include the wall displays of framed pictures of Birmingham airfields; the Alabama National Guard; Women in Aviation; Naval Air Station (NAS) Birmingham; hundreds of framed photos of historic aircraft scattered throughout the museum; selections from the display cases of members of the Alabama Aviation Hall of Fame; and special topics such as the Bay of Pigs or Charles Lindbergh. Of course, the sampling does not include other holdings of the Museum including three dozen aircraft, 50 engines, 200 models, and several hundred paintings.

The coverage was enhanced by copies of photographs from Alvin W. Hudson's collections on Fairgrounds Air Shows, Roberts Field, and the Birmingham Municipal Airport; Cecil Greene's collection on the Alabama National Guard; and individual friends of the Museum who dug up photos of themselves flying in a war or a civilian airplane they once owned. These copies were credited to them herein, but will become a part of the holdings of the Museum. In the same category are personal copies of photographs acquired over 30 years researching and teaching Southern and military history, and working as an Air Force research historian, which were recorded as SMF photos. Finally, a special Women's Auxiliary Ferrying Squadron (WAFS) SMF symposium, attended by six of the surviving nine members of Nancy Love's "Original 25" women flyers in WW II, yielded numerous photographs of this remarkable group. When several clear photographs were available on the same topic, a selection priority was followed to emphasize shots where people were included and ones of general interest over technical. The nature of the available photographs and the *Images of America* series objectives suggested a book for a general audience with broad interests rather than one targeted only to aviation enthusiasts. Hopefully you will find it a good read and good look that will encourage further reading and prompt repeated visits to the Southern Museum of Flight and other aviation museums.

Don and Amy Dodd
Birmingham, Alabama
1999

One

FAIRGROUNDS
AIR SHOWS AND
HEADLESS PUSHERS

Seen here is an aircraft reportedly built in a vacant store on 20th Street North in Birmingham, c. 1912. The street scene depicted above is on 22nd Street looking north from 4th Alley North. (Courtesy of Alvin W. Hudson.)

A Curtiss Model D Type IV "Pusher," 1911–1912, was the first American-made plane to use ailerons. (SMF photo.)

Ruth Law, by flying this Curtiss "Headless" about 1912, became the first woman to fly an Army airplane. (SMF photo.)

A *c.* 1912 Curtiss D-4 Pusher replica at the Southern Museum of Flight is on loan from George Epps. (Courtesy of Bob Kendrick.)

The SMF's Pusher replica was built by John Pruitt and used some original parts including the fuel tank, spruce struts between the wings, and the wooden rudder bar. (Courtesy of Bob Kendrick.)

These early aircraft were photographed at the 1912 Birmingham Fairgrounds Air Show. (Courtesy of Alvin W. Hudson.)

A flying demonstration at the 1915 Birmingham Fairgrounds Air Show is pictured here. (Courtesy of Alvin W. Hudson.)

In this photograph of the 1915 Birmingham Fairgrounds Air Show, the old horse-racing stands can be seen on the left. Vulcan's head and extended right arm are barely visible over the top wing of the plane. (Courtesy of Alvin W. Hudson.)

Stunt pilot Jersey Ringel poses with the Premo Race Car built by Preston Motors Corporation of Birmingham. This photograph was made on September 24, 1921, during the State Fair. (Courtesy of Alvin W. Hudson.)

E.T. Odum's flying machine is displayed at the 1909 Alabama State Fair. (SMF photo.)

14

Walter J. Carr, aviator, flight instructor, inventor, and stunt flyer booked exhibitions through the American Aeroplane Exhibition Company of Humboldt, Tennessee. (SMF photo.)

This photo of Walter J. Carr was taken on June 15, 1914. (SMF photo.)

Lt. James A Meissner stands by his Nieuport 28 on May 30, 1918, after his 2nd confirmed victory. He was a member of the "Hat in the Ring" 94th Aero Squadron based at Gengoult Airfield, in Toul, France. (Courtesy of Alabama Aviation Hall of Fame—AAHOF.)

Pictured is the 94th Aero Squadron, 1st Pursuit Group pilots, in May of 1918 in Toul, France. Meissner is in the second row, third from the right. Standing next to him is Eddie Rickenbacker, the top American Ace in World War I. (Courtesy of AAHOF.)

The 147th Aero Squadron, 1st Pursuit Group officers at Rembercourt Airfield in France are in front of a Spad XIII, in October of 1918. The 1st Group CO, Major Harold E. Hartney, is holding the propeller, and Major James Meissner, the Squadron commander, is next to him on Hartney's left. (Courtesy of AAHOF.)

Lt. William Terry Badham of Birmingham flew as a backseater (observer, photographer, gunner) in the 91st Aero Squadron, Air Service in World War I. In September and October 1918, he shared in the destruction of five German airplanes to become a WW I Ace. In this photo, he is second from the right. (Courtesy of Kyle Badham Long.)

After WW I, Badham started a chemical business and invented a new process for refining naphthalene from crude tar oils. The profits from this patent allowed him the leisure to paint from his mountain retreat at Mentone, Alabama, with regular trips to Mexico and France. He published a book of his watercolors with a brief account of his WW I experiences shortly before his death. (Courtesy of Kyle Badham Long.)

Two

BIRMINGHAM
AIRFIELDS AND A MAN
NAMED MESSER

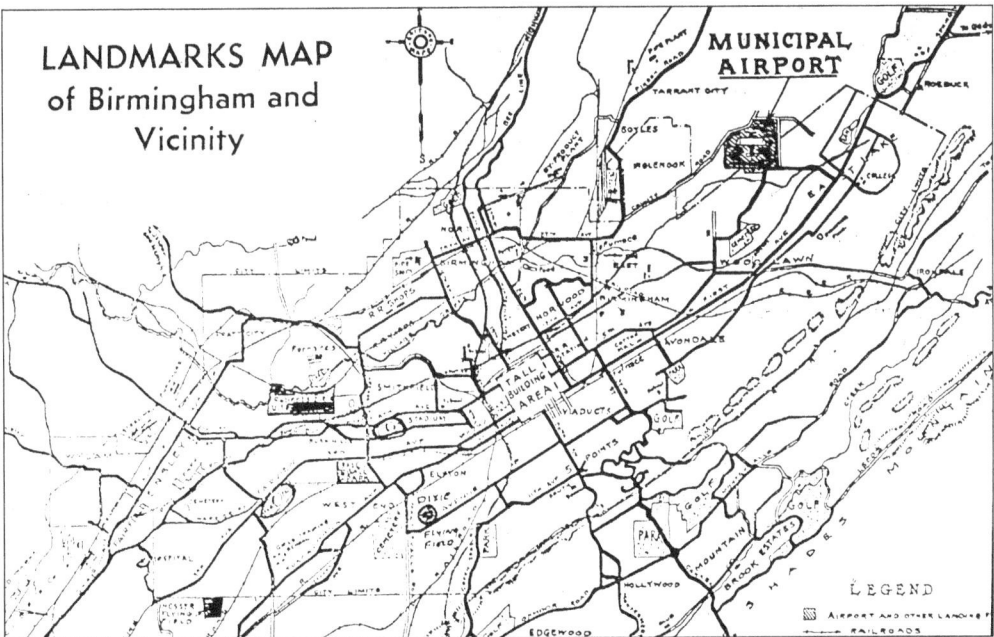

This rough map shows the locations of four Birmingham airfields: Messer Field (later named Central Park Field) in the bottom left, Dixie Field to the northeast (where Loveman's Village is now located across from Elmwood Cemetery), Roberts Field to the north (west of Birmingham), and the Birmingham Municipal Airport to the northeast. (SMF map.)

Virgil Evans was the builder of Dixie Field, the first airport in Birmingham, in 1920. (SMF photo.)

The buildings and flight line, including an advertisement for flying lessons, are shown at Dixie Field. (SMF photo.)

20

Glenn Messer is shown in front of a Curtiss JN "Jenny" in 1924. The "Jenny" was the most used trainer by U.S. and Canadian WW I crews— 6,400 were built. Although the U.S. military used the plane until 1927, most were sold after WW I. It became a favorite of barnstormers of the 1920s such as Messer, Phoebe Fairgrave Omlie, and Bessie Coleman. (SMF photo.)

A Curtiss JN-4D "Jenny" airplane is shown on a small field behind East Lake Park in 1924. The automobile parked beside the plane is an "Essex" 4. (SMF photo.)

Elmer Walker was chief mechanic at Dixie Flying Field. (SMF photo.)

JN-4Ds and a "Canuck" rest along the flight line. (SMF photo.)

A Curtiss JN-4D demonstrates one of the sources of revenue for early aviation operators. (SMF photo.)

Some of the pets kept at Dixie Flying Field amuse a young lady. (SMF photo.)

A Curtiss JN-4 "Jenny" sits next to a "Star" automobile. (SMF photo.)

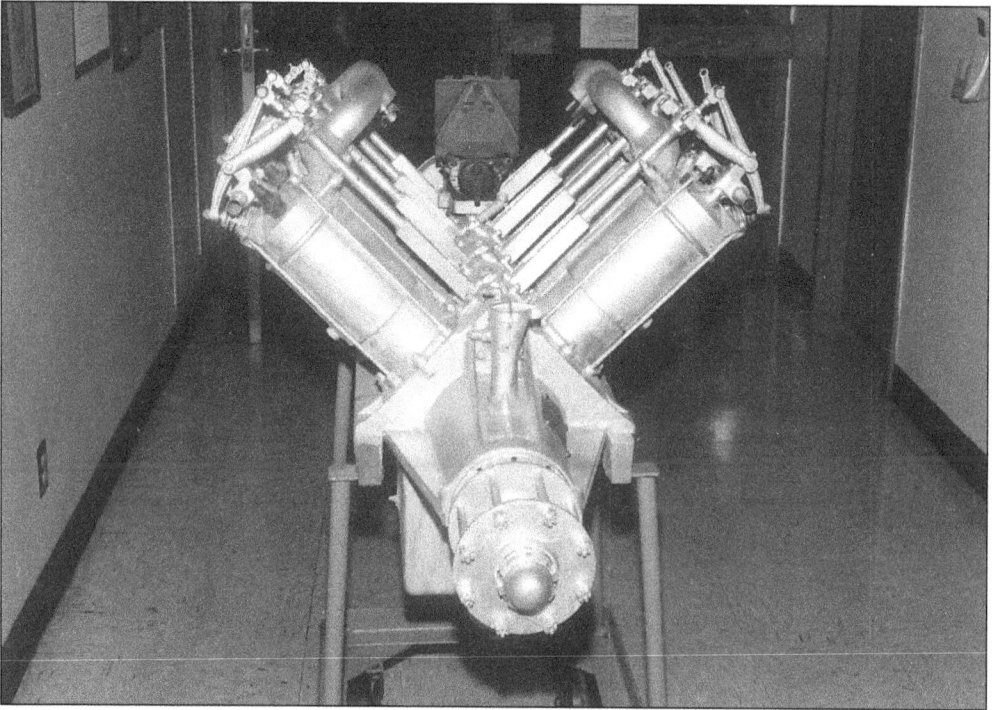

In the SMF collection is this 90 HP OX-5 engine that powered the "Jenny." (SMF photo.)

This 1920s airship visitor to Roberts Field is possibly the U.S. Navy Zeppelin ZR-1 "Shenandoah," which came to Birmingham in 1924. (SMF photo.)

Anthony H.G. Fokker designed the Fokker D-7 and the Fokker Tri-Plane of WW I. He also designed and built private, military, and airline aircraft in the United States and Canada after the war. See page 63 for a Museum aircraft designed by Fokker. (SMF photo.)

Messer Field was constructed by Glenn Messer in 1926–1927. He was the operator until it became Central Park Field in 1935. (SMF photo.)

A Ford Tri-Motor visited Messer Field in 1929. Henry Ford bought the Stout Metal Airplane Company in 1925 and produced three-engine commercial monoplanes until 1933. At the time of this visit, Ford was turning out four "Tin Goose" Tri-Motors a week. (SMF photo.)

An Air Boss, Waco 10, and Swallow rest at Messer Field. The Swallow Aeroplane Company was the successor to the E.M. Laird Company, and this Swallow is probably the commercial three-seater (refined Laird Swallow), a popular passenger-carrier in the Midwest. (SMF photo.)

When Waco Aircraft Corporation was formed from Advance Aircraft Company in 1929, it was the largest producer of commercial aircraft in the U.S., possibly greater than all other U.S. competitors combined. This Waco 10 was photographed at Messer Field in 1933. (SMF photo.)

Glenn Messer, airport owner and operator, airplane designer and builder, flying circus co-owner, Early Bird pilot (organization of pilots who soloed before December 17, 1916), and inventor, was a Birmingham legend. He was known for his daredevil stunts depicted in the following photographs. (SMF photo.)

In this photo, Messer is preparing to hang by his teeth to a leather strap. The strap, a rope ladder, and other Messer paraphernalia are displayed in the Museum. (SMF photo.)

Flying circus performers operating outside the airplane while it was in flight were commonly known as "wing-walkers." Messer fulfills the image in this photo, displayed at the Museum. (SMF photo.)

Only the tallest wing-walkers could perform this Messer maneuver of hanging upside down between the wings. (SMF photo.)

Glenn Messer designed the "Air Boss," which was manufactured by Southern Aircraft Corporation in Birmingham, Alabama, from 1926 to 1930. (SMF postcard.)

Seen here is the cockpit of Messer's Air Boss in 1929. (SMF photo.)

Glenn Messer is sitting on the running board of a 1926–1927 Pierce-Arrow. Appropriately buried on a hillside overlooking the Birmingham International Airport, Messer's tombstone inscription reads: "Glenn E. Messer, Sr., July 12, 1895–June 13, 1995, A life devoted to the development of aviation since 1911." (SMF photo.)

Phoebe Fairgrave Omlie operated a "Flying Circus" with Glenn Messer in the mid-1920s. A noted skydiver and flying-school owner, she conceived the plan to paint town names and directional indicators on the roofs of buildings throughout the United States. With the assistance of Eleanor Roosevelt, some women fliers were employed to scout the air routes. Eventually 16,000 markers—one every 15 miles on every U.S. air route—were painted. (SMF photo.)

Katherine Stinson of the Stinson School of Flying in San Antonio, Texas, had a sister and two brothers who were pilots. In 1916–1917, the petite Katherine toured Japan and China to appreciative audiences, especially women. Her first Tokyo appearance drew 25,000 spectators. (SMF photo.)

A Mrs. Moon stands on the wing of her plane at Central Park Field in 1946. (Courtesy of Alvin W. Hudson).

Central Park Field (1934–1946) was operated by Mrs. Grace Bailey. A hanger and aerial view of the airfield are shown here. (SMF photos.)

Roberts Field (1922–1950), located west of downtown Birmingham along Village Creek, was the first city-owned airport. The field was named for Lt. Meredith Roberts of Birmingham, who was killed in WW I. Except for a period during WW II when military pilots trained there, Roberts was a civilian field until it closed in 1950. This photo was taken in 1930. (SMF photo.)

Vivian Jones flies a Curtiss JN-4 "Jenny" over the Fairfield Iron Works in 1928. (SMF photo.)

Roy P. Bridges, pictured in 1929, was a well-known civilian/sportsman pilot, Aeronauts Club leader, BAC member, and owner of Birmingham Automobile dealerships including Austin, Nash, Willys, and Volkswagen. (SMF photo.)

This Travel Air 400, powered by a 220 HP Wright J-5 engine, of the St. Tammany Gulf Coast Airways Incorporated, carried U.S. mail and passengers between Birmingham and Atlanta, linking New York and New Orleans in 1928. (Courtesy Cecil Greene.)

Located at Roberts Field, this wooden structure photographed in the mid-1920s, housed the 106th Observation Squadron Headquarters, Alabama National Guard. (Courtesy of Alvin W. Hudson.)

Several men work at refueling a Ford Tri-Motor. When the photo was taken in 1930, fuel was hand pumped from the tank truck into the plane. (SMF photo.)

Richard Evelyn Byrd (1888–1957), Naval Academy graduate of 1912 and naval aviator, took part in the 1914 Vera Cruz, Mexico mission, and commanded a Navy patrol squadron based in Canada during WW I. He is best known for his polar expeditions highlighted by the first flights over the North Pole in May 1926 and the South Pole in November 1929. These photos were taken when he visited Birmingham in April of 1929. (SMF photos.)

"Hap Hazard" and his Travel-Air stunt plane were photographed in 1930. (SMF photo.)

The Ford Tri-Motor 4-AT-B was powered by three Wright J-5 engines at 220 HP each. This photo was taken in 1928. (SMF photo.)

Baby Ruth candy, advertised here, was named for the daughter of President Grover and Frances Folsom Cleveland, who was born in the White House. (SMF photo.)

Instructor Chuck Hale congratulates a new pilot on his first solo in an Ercoupe. (SMF photo.)

Built in Saginaw, Michigan, by Walter J. Carr, the 1929 Paramount "Cabinaire" was one of the first cabin bi-planes to carry four people. Powered by a 165 HP Wright J-6 engine, it cruised at just over 100 miles per hour. The initial cost was $7,500. (SMF photo.)

On April 1, 1935, Leo Thompson of Clanton, Alabama, accomplishes his first solo flight in a 1930 Aeronca C-3, powered by a 36 HP Aeronca engine. "Alka-Seltzer" was good for upset stomachs then, too! (SMF photo.)

The "Pride of the 12th Annual National Air Carnival" was photographed at Roberts Field in the spring of 1946. (SMF photo.)

"Sky-Writing and Banner-Towing" were advertised in this 1946 photograph made at Roberts Field. (SMF photo.)

A small collection of buildings served as the operations office at Roberts Field on August 31, 1946. (SMF photo.)

This aerial view of Roberts Field was taken in 1948, about two years before the field closed. (SMF photo.)

The Airdrome, located at Roberts Field, was a popular restaurant/night club in the late 1940s and early 1950s. (SMF photo.)

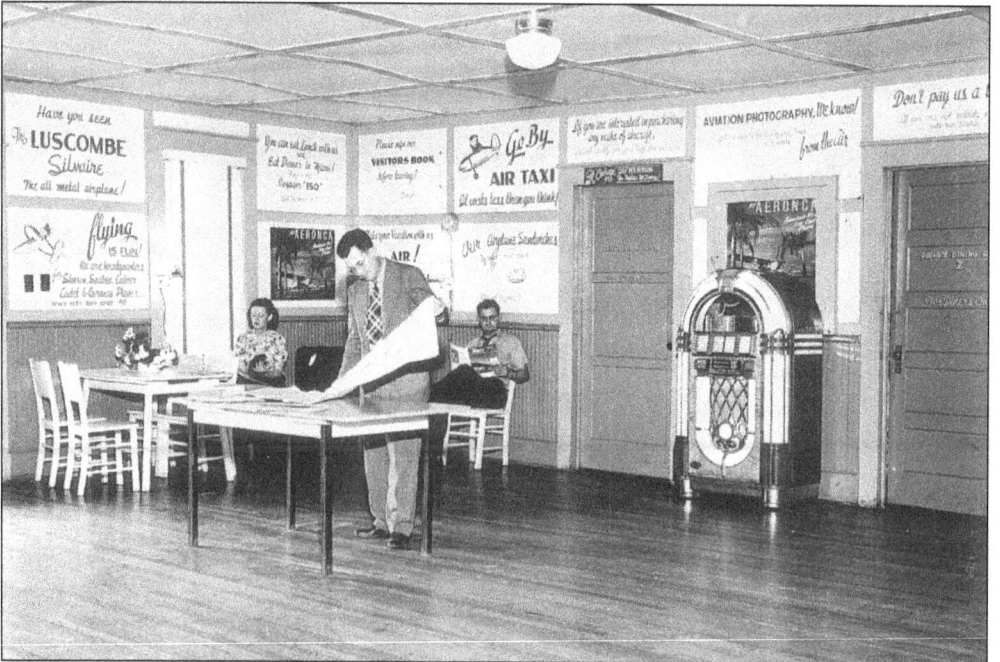

Inside the Airdrome, local businesses found available advertising space on the walls. (Courtesy of Alvin W. Hudson.)

44

Seen here is an aerial look at Roberts Field before Interstate 20/59 was built. (Courtesy of Alvin W. Hudson.)

Construction work on Interstate 20/59 is shown on the lower right side of this photo. (Courtesy of Alvin W. Hudson.)

This 1928 production model of the long-wing Alexander Eaglerock, designed by 19-year-old Al Mooney, had a longer lower wing to get it off the ground sooner. On loan from George Epps, the Museum's long-wing is one of five known to exist. (Courtesy of Bob Kendrick.)

Three

ROBERTS FIELD, THE GUARD, AND THE LONE EAGLE

Roberts Field was the first home of the Alabama Guard, 106th Observation Squadron. Pilots of the 106th Squadron pictured, from left to right, are: (front row) Lts. Jerry Thomas, unidentified, Henry Badham, Walter Wise, unidentified, Kirkpatrick, Clifton Stephenson, P.H. Barnett, and Vivian Jones; (back row) Capt. Meadow, Lt. Newberger, Capt. John Donelson, Lt. Johnny Gill, and Maj. Sumpter Smith. (SMF photo.)

An aerial view of the Birmingham skyline was made by the 106th Observation Squadron, Alabama National Guard, in 1928. (Courtesy of Cecil Greene.)

ROSTER
106TH OBSERVATION SQUADRON, ALABAMA NATIONAL GUARD

HIS EXCELLENCY, COL. BIBB GRAVES   GOVERNOR OF ALABAMA
GEN. F. E. BUTLER   THE ADJUTANT GENERAL
LT. LLOYD BARNETT   REGULAR ARMY INSTRUCTOR
MAJOR SUMPTER SMITH   COMMANDING OFFICER

CAPT. K. D. BRABSTON	1ST LT. C. A. JONES JR.	2ND LT. F. A. STONE
CAPT. E. W. BULLOCK	1ST LT. J. V. THOMAS	2ND LT. A. D. STAFFORD
CAPT. C. A. BARINOWSKI	1ST LT. R. M. GOODALL	2ND LT. A. M. LAGRANGE
CAPT. W. H. BEATTY	1ST LT. J. F. GILL	2ND LT. B. G. THELE
CAPT. H. M. SMITH	1ST LT. H. R. MULL	2ND LT. G. R. BYRUM, JR.
1ST LT. H. L. BADHAM, JR.	1ST LT. E. C. ARMES	2ND LT. F. C. LAW
1ST LT. J. H. WILLIS	1ST LT. L. W. MEADOWS	2ND LT. R. W. GREEN
1ST LT. D. C. BEATTY	2ND LT. T. W. NEWTON	2ND LT. J. A. MEISSNER
1ST LT. P. H. BLACKWELL	2ND LT. C. STEPHENSON	

SERGEANTS

D. B. McCRACKEN	V. W. SMITH	E. G. ADAMS
W. W. WISE	R. O. PAXTON	R. E. GILL
V. B. McCRACKEN	M. B. PARSONS	J. H. MATTHEWS
ELMER WALKER	J. T. FINLEY	G. E. ELLIS
R. H. SNAPP	J. O. FOSTER	D. M. FLOURNEY
G. W. BURT	J. B. THOMAS	E. C. HODGES
T. C. BAGLEY	W. M. COLEMAN	H. P. PETITE
T. E. WHITSON	J. D. WOODWARD	R. J. THOMAS
D. T. LEVERETTE	E. C. BROWN	F. M. DAVIS
W. S. CARLTON	L. N. JOHNSON	

CORPORALS

V. A. SMITH	A. E. DURAN	D. W. THOMAS
J. A. GRYDER	G. K. McWILLIAMS	A. T. REEVES

PRIVATES

J. E. CARDWELL	H. F. DAVIS	G. W. RIBBLE JR.
J. D. DANIELS	F. J. DIGGLE	ALLEN RUSHTON
W. H. DANIELS	W. P. GOLSON JR.	C. T. ROGERS
L. L. DONALDSON	G. R. HARWELL	E. M. RUTZ
W. D. DUPREE	O. W. HECKERT	L. B. SARTAIN, JR.
J. F. KIMBALL	J. L. HODGES, JR.	I. J. SELLERS, JR.
F. L. LAMPMAN	J. P. HORN	A. Y. SHARPE
M. C. THOMPSON	F. M. LYNCH	G. V. SHARPE
S. K. SAWYER	A. R. McBEE	J. B. SPRINGVILLE
O. M. SMITH	T. L. MOSLEY	J. D. SMITH, JR.
I. J. ARMSTRONG JR.	W. D. MURPHY	S. S. TATUM
R. J. BLACKMAN	P. E. MYERS	P. N. WILSON
C. L. BROWN	C. T. PARR	HAMMOND WOOD
S. L. BULLOCK	W. R. PARSONS	J. W. WOLTERSDORF
W. O. CARROLL	E. A. PHILLIPS	J. R. YARBROUGH
C. W. COBB	SIMON PIERCE	F. J. WULLENBUCHER
J. R. COLLINS	W. F. RAWSON	M. B. CLAYTON
S. M. CRUMRINE	WALTER RAY	
E. R. DAVIS		

106TH PHOTO SECTION   1ST LT. V. M. JONES, C. O.

SGT. W. L. BLOODWORTH	SGT. J. J. HUGHES	SGT. J. W. ECHELS
SGT. A. D. FLEMING	SGT. R. G. THELE	

PRIVATES

C. H. BROWN	D. C. DELANY	C. R. MURTON

The 1928 Roster contains the names of the members when the 106th Observation Squadron was based at Roberts Field. In 1931, the Guard moved to the Birmingham Municipal Airport. (Courtesy of Cecil Greene.)

Colonel Sumpter Smith, seen in this 1932 photograph, was Commanding Officer of the 106th Observation Squadron, Alabama National Guard. (SMF photo.)

In the forward cockpit is 1st Lt. Don Beatty. Behind him is 2nd Lt. Clifton Stephenson. (Courtesy of Cecil Greene.)

Pictured here is early Guard pilot Captain K.D. Brabston. In civilian life, Kenneth was a salesman for Henry G. Brabston & Co. (Courtesy of Cecil Greene.)

Lts. Paul Blackwell and Fraser Law (above) were among the earliest Guard pilots. Blackwell, a TCI employee, attended primary flying school with Lindbergh in San Antonio. Law worked for Alabama Power. (Courtesy of Cecil Greene.)

Alabama National Guard personnel are pictured on March 19, 1929. (SMF photo.)

Capt. William H. Beatty. (SMF photo.)

Officers of the 106th Observation Squadron pose at Wilder Field, Georgia, on August 22, 1934. (SMF photo.)

The Douglas O-38 was an improved model of the Douglas observation biplane and powered by a 525 HP Pratt and Whitney R-1690-5 Hornet radial engine. (SMF photo.)

The Curtiss O-11 was a Liberty-powered version of a Curtiss O-1G (similar to the O-1B). Sixty-six were built for National Guard use. (Courtesy of Cecil Greene.)

A Douglas O-2 Guard aircraft flies over southwest Birmingham on June 3, 1936. (SMF photo.)

Guard mechanics Bob Kirkley and Jim Foster pose with their Douglas O2-H aircraft. (SMF photo.)

The National Guard buildings at Roberts Field are visible in this July 7, 1935 aerial shot. (SMF photo.)

Roberts Field fellows admire *Miss Birmingham* in the 1920s. (Courtesy of Cecil Greene.)

Charles Augustus Lindbergh (1902–1974) had several Alabama "connections." He bought his first plane, a "Jenny," from Glenn Messer and, in being oriented to the plane, perhaps soloed for the first time. He barnstormed Alabama in 1924 and his father had a half-brother, Augustus, who had worked for Frisco Railroad in western Jefferson County. (SMF photo.)

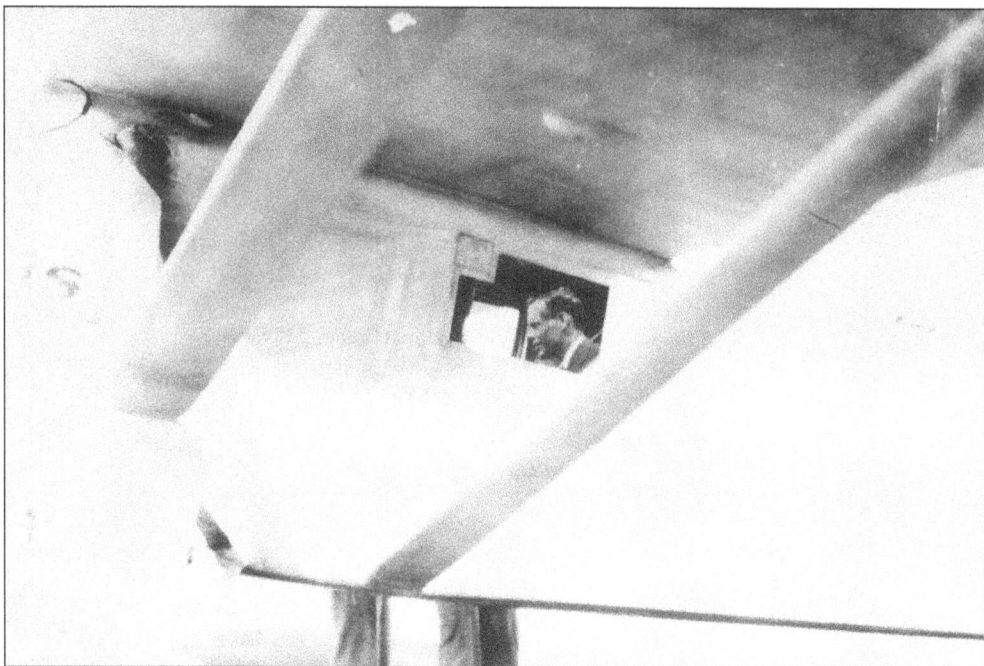
Lindbergh arrives at Roberts Field, 1927. (SMF photos.)

Lindbergh's Birmingham visit in October 1927 was a part of his nationwide tour promoting aviation coast-to-coast on the heels of his historic New York to Paris trans-Atlantic flight of 1927. (SMF photo.)

The crowd rushes to get a glimpse of Lindbergh as the *Spirit of St. Louis* is moved into the National Guard hangar at Roberts Field. (Courtesy of Cecil Greene.)

Lindbergh is escorted by Alabama Guard Major, Sumpter Smith. Just after Lindy's famous flight, Smith flew non-stop from Birmingham to Washington, D.C., proving the feasibility of an air mail route that began in 1928. (SMF photo.)

A banquet was given for the "Lone Eagle" in Birmingham. Pictured at the head table, from left to right, are: Mrs. Bibb Graves, Commission President J.M. Jones Jr., Mrs. Sumpter Smith, Lindbergh, Hugh Morrow, Maj. Sumpter Smith, and Gov. Bibb Graves. (SMF photo.)

Lindbergh returns to Birmingham a few months before his death in 1974 and meets with local aviation dignitaries. Pictured from left to right are: (front row) Bill Franklin, Hoyt Sargeant, Lindbergh, and Jerry Thomas; (back row) Paul Graham, Joe Shannon, John Donalson, Larry Brabham, David Whiteside, and Mitchell Joseph. (SMF photo.)

Amelia Earhart is shown with Hollywood stunt man Paul Mantz and Marshall Headle. (SMF photo.)

Amelia Earhart, Wiley Post, and Roscoe Turner look over the latest Pratt and Whitney engine. Post was a noted round-the-world pilot and pioneered high altitude flying. He was killed along with humorist Will Rogers at Point Barrow, Alaska, in 1935. Roscoe Turner was the only racing pilot to win the Thompson Race three times in a row. (SMF photo.)

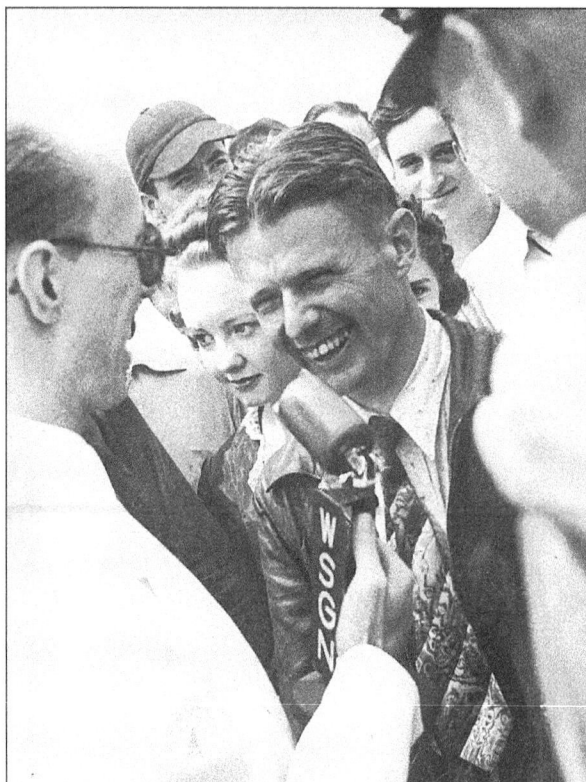

WSGN announcer interviews Douglas "Wrong Way" Corrigan at Birmingham after his flight from New York to Ireland in 1938. (SMF photo.)

The Huff-Daland cropduster, designed by Tony Fokker, was the "Puffer" of choice for Delta Air Corporation, which evolved into Delta Airlines. (SMF photo.)

The Southern Museum of Flight "Puffer" used the popular J-5 Wright Whirlwind engine similar to the engine on Lindbergh's *Spirit of St. Louis* Ryan. (Courtesy of Bob Kendrick.)

Delta Passenger service was inaugurated in 1929 with single-engine, 90-mile-per hour Travelaire aircraft. Standing with a group of employees, second from left, is C. E. Woolman, principal founder of Delta.

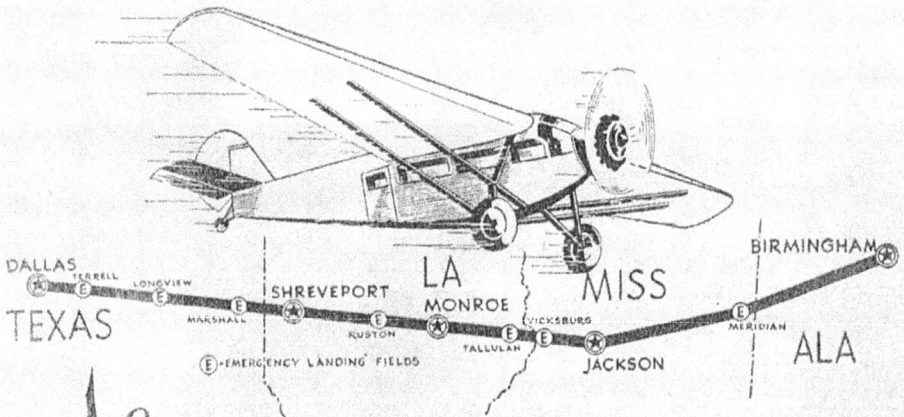

An early ad in 1929 shows the Travelaire on Delta's Trans-Southern route.

This 1927 ad shows Delta's earliest passenger service with its "Travelaire." The Travel Air Manufacturing Company was formed by Walter Beech, Clyde Cessna, and Lloyd Stearman in 1924, but absorbed by Curtiss-Wright in 1929. (SMF photo.)

Four

A NEW AIRPORT, NATIONAL AIR CARNIVALS, AND WW II

One of the most beautiful air terminals in the United States graced the Birmingham Municipal Airport from its founding in 1931 to the post-WW II era. Southern Airways, Delta, Capital, and Eastern passengers were served by a restaurant at one end and an emergency hospital room on the other. Observation platforms were built for airplane watching. The manager's quarters were upstairs. (SMF photo.)

Rocking chairs on the porch of the Birmingham Air Terminal suggest a less hectic time. It is hard to believe that almost three million folks passed through the modern Birmingham International Airport (BIA) in 1998. (Courtesy of Alvin W. Hudson.)

Steadham Acker (1896–1952) was known as "Mr. American Aviation," for air show promotion and especially for spearheading the highly successful annual National Air Carnival at the Birmingham Municipal Airport. He managed the airport from its beginning in 1931 to 1944. (SMF photo.)

A 1936 snowstorm closed the airport and most Birmingham roads as the city reportedly received 13 inches of snow. (Courtesy of Alvin W. Hudson.)

Frank Hulse, president of Southern Airways, with general offices in the building below, announced in 1949 that Southern had service to 20 Southern cities—from Memphis to the west, Charlotte to the east, and Jacksonville, Florida, to the south. Atlanta was the center of the system. Macon, Augusta, and Charleston were served through Columbus, Georgia. (top—SMF photo; bottom—courtesy of Alvin W. Hudson.)

Miss Southern Airways became Miss American Aviation in 1953, and Southern Airways had a promotional picture. (Courtesy of Alvin W. Hudson.)

Delta began service from Dallas to Birmingham in 1929 and on to Atlanta by 1930. When the Air Terminal opened in 1931, Delta was ready. (Courtesy of Alvin W. Hudson.)

Note the interesting dress of these late 1940s Eastern Airlines passengers and the method of boarding. The Air Terminal and Southern Airways hangar is in the background. (Courtesy of Alvin W. Hudson.)

This 1951 photo highlights the airport service of the Whitman Cab Company. (Courtesy of Alvin W. Hudson.)

Eastern Airlines' Eddie Rickenback comes to Birmingham Municipal Airport in the early 1950s. Eva Fitch, widow of Jack Bishop of Eastern, thinks the two men flanking Rickenback are his sons, and the man on the extreme right is Eastern's Bev Griffith. (Courtesy of Alvin W. Hudson.)

Hollywood movie director Henry King participated in the 1940 National Air Carnival. (SMF photo.)

The Birmingham Air Terminal and vicinity is lined with spectators viewing a mid-1930s airshow. (Courtesy of Alvin W. Hudson.)

A Douglas DC-2 is visible in front of the Air Terminal during the 1939 National Air Carnival. (SMF photo.)

Harold Wood sports a new WACO for the 1940 National Air Carnival. The Carnival was suspended during WW II, but resumed in 1946. (SMF photo.)

The official host of the 1946 National Air Carnival was Hollywood's Buddy Rogers, a pilot and husband of actress Mary Pickford. Rogers is seen here riding in a convertible with Miss American Aviation 1946. The Carnival attracted 400,000 spectators in two days and made *Ripley's Believe It Or Not.* (Courtesy of Alvin W. Hudson.)

Aircraft line the edge of the Birmingham Municipal Airport runways, and the crowd concentrates around the air terminal for this 1930s air show. (SMF photo.)

Teresa James flies the first air mail out of Wilkensburg, Pennsylvania, in May 1938. (Courtesy of Teresa James.)

Teresa James, Barbara Poole, and other women pilots of WW II accumulated flying hours by "barnstorming" before the war. Teresa James is the featured "Girl Stunt Pilot" in this 1935 air show advertisement. (Courtesy of Teresa James.)

Miss Eva Parrish of Excel, Alabama, was a nurse at South Highlands Infirmary and a night student at Howard College (Eastlake) when she was selected to be one of the first nine Delta Airlines stewardesses. She worked five days, was off for three, and was paid $110 a month plus expenses. (Courtesy of Mrs. Eva Fitch.)

Mrs. Eva Bishop Fitch returned to Atlanta for a reunion of the "original nine" and was photographed with Delta founder and President C.E. Woolman. (Courtesy of Mrs. Eva Fitch.)

Boeing built 162 of the above P-26A "Pea Shooters." It and the B-10B Martin bomber below both made the recent "Classic Aircraft" list of the Postal Service. (SMF photo.)

Martin built 103 of the B-10B bombers whose maximum speed was 212 miles per hour, only 22 miles per hour slower than the pursuit plane above. (SMF photo.)

The C-47 Skytrain (DC-3 commercial, Navy R4D, British "Dakota") was considered by Eisenhower to be one of the four most significant weapons of WW II. As DC-3s, they formed the nucleus of the post-WW II airline fleets. C-47s played a major role in the Berlin Airlift and were used as transports in Korea and gunships in Vietnam. The "Gooney Bird" still flies, as seen below. (SMF photo.)

The Southern Museum of Flight's Skytrain is shown with C-47 qualified pilots Alan Henley, Dudley Pewitt, and Mark Henley. (SMF photo.)

Stearman built about 10,000 two-seat primary trainers for the Navy and U.S. Army Air Corps from 1934 through WW II. A Stearman-Boeing PT-17 "Kaydet" is shown above. (SMF photo.)

T-6 flown by Alan, Mark, or Tom Henley in the Annual Fall Birmingham Aero Club Airshow at Bessemer Airport. (Courtesy of Mark Henley.)

The Southern Museum of Flight's BT-13 basic trainer arrived via Les Chapman's truck (above) and members of the Experimental Aircraft Association (EAA) looked it over (below). Pictured from left to right are: John Burgin, Roy Pounds, Larry Tillery (in cockpit), Dave Callahan, Jack Gerhart, and Raymon Ross. (SMF photo.)

The AT-6 Texan was called the "Harvard" by the British and designated the "SNJ" by the Navy. It has a maximum speed of 200 miles per hour and cruise speed of 160 miles per hour. (SMF photo.)

The North American AT (Advanced Trainer)-6 of WW II, with a 600 HP Pratt and Whitney radial engine, handled like a fighter, as Alan Henley's "North American Team" demonstrates at the annual Birmingham Aero Club Airshow. The SMFs AT-6 is the gift of Clyde Cox. (Courtesy of Bob Kendrick.)

Dignitaries attending the 1939 or 1940 National Air Carnival include, from left to right: Governor Frank Dixon, Mayor Jimmie Morgan, Airport Manager Steadham Acker, NBC's "Breakfast Club" host Don McNeil, WSGN Program Director Bob McRaney, and Tutwiler Hotel Manager Burt Orndorff. (SMF photo.)

Alabama's "Flying Governor," Chauncey Sparks (center), is welcomed to Birmingham in 1943 by Birmingham Aero Club (BAC) President Dan Hudson (left) and the president of the Birmingham City Commission, W. Cooper Green (right). All three were BAC members as was their pilot, Major Harold Wood, CAP Wing Commander. (SMF photo.)

Col. John M. Donalson, CO, 438th Troop Carrier Group, 9th AF (photo below), piloted the Douglas C-47A *Belle of Birmingham* as the lead aircraft of the airborne invasion of Europe on D-Day, June 6, 1944—the Normandy invasion. (SMF photos.)

Joe Shannon, with his P-38 Lightning in WW II, served with the 97th Fighter Squadron, 82nd Fighter Group. He later flew a B-25 Mitchell in the China-Burma-India Theater. (Courtesy of Joe Shannon.)

Piloted by Joe Shannon, this P-38 was the first aircraft to land safely in the invasion of Italy. Joe's wingman landed first but crashed into the water tank truck in the background. (Courtesy of Joe Shannon.)

Bill Barnes was a P-38 pilot in WW II flying with the 20th Fighter Group, 8th Air Force, from Kings Cliffe, England. (Courtesy of Bill Barnes.)

R.L. Pinson (in photo) was Line Chief for Anniston's Gus Leslie, who dubbed his P-51 Mustang of the 343rd Fighter Squadron, 55th Fighter Group, the "Bama Blitz." (Courtesy of Bill Chambless.)

Gen. Robert D. Knapp (top row, second from left) of Auburn, Alabama, was CO of the 57th Bomb Wing in WW II. One of "his boys" wrote of his leadership: "He taught his men that the measure of every man's virtue is best revealed in time of adversity, adversity that does not weaken a man but rather shows what he is." (SMF photo.)

The WACO CG-4A was the only American-built troop-carrying glider used by allied forces in the airborne invasion of Sicily and France. (Courtesy of Irvin Kinney.)

Irvin Kinney, Citadel graduate with a pilot's license from the Civilian Pilot Training (CPT) program, became a combat glider pilot in WW II and survived missions to Sicily, Holland ("Market Garden"), Germany ("Varsity"), and a one-glider top secret OSS mission into Yugoslavia. Some of his WW II memorabilia is shown here. (Courtesy of Irvin Kinney.)

Lowery "Brab" Brabham resigned from the Army Air Corps, 36th Pursuit Squadron, 8th Group, in July 1940 to be a test pilot for Republic. Six months later, he was Chief Test Pilot. (SMF photo.)

As Chief Test Pilot for Republic, Brabham did the original testing on the P-47 Thunderbolt "Jug" and the XR-12 Rainbow. The Rainbow was an airline aircraft that had a cruise speed of 450 miles per hour and top speed of 500 miles per hour (in 1946!). (SMF photo.)

Charles A. Lindbergh is pictured with Thomas McGuire, P-38 pilot with the 431st Fighter Squadron, 475th Fighter Group, who had 38 air-to-air victories by war's end. Lindbergh taught the P-38 pilots fuel efficiency techniques to get longer ranges with the same amount of fuel. (Courtesy of Jason Frost.)

Rear Admiral John G. Crommelin Jr. was Flight Officer of the aircraft carrier U.S.S. *Enterprise*, the ship with the greatest fighting record of WW II. The Wetumpka native was a major force behind the "Big E's" spirit. With gusto, he led the "Revolt of the Admirals" after the war to save the carrier for the fleet. (Courtesy of AAHOF.)

Norm Ponder of Pelham is completing an 11-foot model of the U.S.S. *Enterprise* for a museum exhibit on naval aviation. Norm earlier did a battleship *Alabama* model for Battleship Park in Mobile, and a wooden Mercedes engine for the museum's Fokker D-VII in restoration. (Courtesy of Norm Ponder.)

Five Crommelin brothers from Wetumpka graduated from the U.S. Naval Academy, and the four profiled herein were naval aviators in WW II. Richard entered combat first, shooting down two Zero fighters in the Battle of the Coral Sea and another in the Battle of Midway. He was killed in a midair collision in 1945. (Courtesy of AAHOF.)

Charles Crommelin graduated from the Naval Academy in 1933 and became a top test pilot. He commanded a squadron, then a group, on the U.S.S. *Yorktown* and was badly wounded. He returned to command Air Group 12, "Crommelin's Thunderbirds." Like Richard (above), he was killed in a midair collision in 1945. (Courtesy of AAHOF.)

Quentin Crommelin graduated from the Academy in 1941 and served on the U.S.S. *Sarotoga* until it was knocked out at Guadalcanal. He returned to the United States for flight training, got his wings, and flew off the aircraft carrier *Antietam*. He was CO of the U.S.S. *Lexington* after the war and retired as a Captain in 1973. (Courtesy of AAHOF.)

David McCampbell of Bessemer, Alabama, graduated from the Naval Academy, became a naval aviator, and commanded Air Group 15 in WW II. During a seven-month combat tour, the group sank more shipping and shot down more enemy aircraft than any group in naval history. McCampbell became the Navy's top ace with 34 victories and was awarded the Medal of Honor. (Courtesy of AAHOF.)

Alabama National Guardsmen fought in the Southwest Pacific in WW II, flying the B-25 Mitchells shown in the photos. They were assigned to the 106th Reconnaissance Squadron. The "Educated Death" guys were members of the photo section caught on camera before leaving for the Southwest Pacific. The "Blue Eyes" fellows were in New Guinea. (SMF photos.)

Brig. Gen. Benjamin O. Davis Sr. greets his son Colonel B.O. Davis Jr. and Staff. Gen. Davis Sr. was the first black general in the Army. After the war, Gen. Davis Jr. became the first black general in the Air Force. (Courtesy of United States Air Force Historical Research Agency—USAFHRA.)

Captain Turner congratulates 2nd Lt. Clarence D. Lester on destroying 3 ME-109's on July 18, 1944, over northern Italy. (Courtesy of USAFHRA.)

Ranking Army Air Force Officials attended a ceremony awarding four 332nd Fighter Group pilots the Distinguished Flying Cross. Dignitaries were, from left to right, Lt. Gen. Ira C. Eaker, Maj. Gen. Nathan F. Twining, Brig. Gen. B.O. Davis Sr., Brig. Gen. Dean C. Strother, and Maj. Nelson S. Brooks. (Courtesy of USAFHRA.)

Capt. Joseph D. Elsberry and Sgt. Joe Louis discuss the Mustang while Joe tries sitting in the cockpit. (Courtesy of USAFHRA.)

After graduating from Tuskegee Institute, James became a Tuskegee Airman and was assigned to the 477th Composite Group, which did not go overseas. He remained in the Air Force and flew over 100 missions in Korea and Vietnam. Afterwards James became the first black four-star General and Commander-in-Chief of the North American Air Defense Command. (Courtesy of USAFHRA.)

In August 1945, Tuskegee Institute hosted an "Anniversary Assembly" celebrating the Tuskegee role in WW II. Distinguished guests, pictured from left to right, included: Col. Eugene H. Dibble, CO Tuskegee Veterans Facility; Col. Noel F. Parrish, CO Tuskegee AAF; Capt. Luke J. Weathers, Instructor, Tuskegee AAF; Col. Benjamin O. Davis Jr., CO Godman Field, Ky.; Dr. Frederick D. Patterson, President, Tuskegee Institute; Col. Richard C. Cumming, Post Surgeon, Tuskegee AAF; and Maj. Howard C. Magoon, CO. 2164th AAF Base Unit, Primary School, Tuskegee Institute, Alabama. (Courtesy of USAFHRA.)

Tuskegee Airman Richard Macon shakes hands with his WW II flight instructor, "Chief" Anderson as Charles Shafer (on the extreme right) looks on. Macon is a former mathematics professor at Miles College where he taught longtime Birmingham mayor Richard Arrington. (Courtesy of Richard Macon.)

Four P-51 pilots of the 332nd Fighter Group reunite in 1972 with a common bond—all were shot down the same day in WW II combat, August 12, 1944, and all survived the experience. Pictured from left to right are, Alexander Jefferson, Robert Daniels, Richard Macon, and Robert O'Neal. The Air Force jet in the background is an F-100 Super Sabre. (Courtesy of Richard Macon.)

Nancy Love suggested women ferrying pilots to the military in 1940 and in 1942 was appointed director of the Women's Auxiliary Ferrying Squadron (WAFS) at New Castle Army Air Base in Wilmington, Delaware. A pilot's pilot, she led by example. Love was one of the first pilots to fly the P-51 and was the first woman to fly the B-17. (Courtesy of Teresa James.)

Betty Gillies was selected to be Nancy Love's executive officer. She was a veteran flyer who had helped Amelia Earhart establish the Ninety-nines (99 of the 117 licensed women pilots were charter members). The WAFS established the following qualifications: a 500-flying-hour minimum, 200 HP experience, a commercial license, a high school education, and references. The age requirements were between 21 and 35. Telegrams were sent to 200 women pilots. One hundred responded and 25 were selected. (Courtesy of Teresa James.)

Barbara Jane "B.J." Erickson (London), WAFS commander at Long Beach, California, is shown with Evelyn Sharp, who was later killed when her P-38 quit during take-off. (Courtesy of B.J. Erickson London.)

WW II fliers sharing experiences are pictured from left to right: Francis S. "Gabe" Gabreski, 61st Fighter Squadron (29 victories); Teresa James, WAFS Ferrying Command pilot; and Robert S. Johnson, 61st and 62nd Fighter Squadrons (27 victories). This photograph was made in London in 1974. (Courtesy of Teresa James.)

The Civilian Pilot Training (CPT) program at the University of Alabama made flying possible for Nancy Batson. She soloed in a Piper Cub, got her private and commercial licenses, and taught flying for Embry-Riddle in Miami. Her first student to solo was Janet Reno's aunt, Winifred Wood. Hearing of Nancy Love's WAFS, Batson quit her job and headed for Delaware. She eventually flew P-38s, P-39s, P-40s, P-47s, and P-51s. (Courtesy of Nancy Batson Crews.)

Nancy Batson Crews sits in the cockpit of an AT-6 Texan, perhaps recalling her instrument training in the same aircraft. Her instructor was a quiet but professional man who later got into politics in Arizona—Barry Goldwater. (Courtesy of Nancy Crews.)

Nancy stands by a P-38 packing a .45 pistol on her right hip. Once while ferrying a P-38 from Pittsburgh to Newark, she may have wished for a weapon to use on the landing gear. The nose gear wouldn't go down. After circling the field for two hours pumping the pressure by hand, and blistering her hand badly in the process, she finally blew it out. Not knowing whether the nose gear was rigidly locked, she landed nose up and eased it down. Then she noticed a parade of emergency vehicles following her down the runway. A young man climbed up the wing and asked her to get out so he could taxi to a hangar. The plucky Nancy retorted abruptly, "If I can get it this far, I think I can handle the taxiing." (Courtesy of Nancy Crews.)

WAFS pilots studying maps prior to a ferrying mission are from left to right: Gertrude Meserve (Tubbs), Nancy Batson (Crews), Teresa James, Esther Nelson, Dorothy Fulton, and (kneeling) Betty Gillies, commander of the WAFS for the 2nd Ferrying Group, Wilmington, Delaware. (Courtesy of Nancy Crews.)

WAFS snowbound in Montana include from left to right, Nancy Batson (Crews), Phyllis Burchfield, Delphine Bohn (Squadron CO), Kathryn Rawls (1930s Olympic swimmer), and Florene Miller (Watson). (Courtesy of Nancy Crews.)

WAFS pilot Teresa James waves prior to takeoff from Farmingdale, New York, in September 1944, to ferry the 10,000th Thunderbolt produced by Republic, 1942–1944. (Courtesy of Teresa James.)

Teresa James became the first WAFS pilot to ferry an aircraft coast-to-coast. She delivered a Fairchild PT-19 "Cornell" trainer from Hagerstown, Maryland, to Burbank, California, in 1943. The PT-19 was used in the film *Ladies Courageous* starring Loretta Young as Nancy Love, CO of the WAFS. After the flight, Teresa had coffee with Bob Hope at the Brown Derby in Hollywood. (Courtesy of Teresa James.)

WAFS pilots, pictured from left to right, Dorothy Fulton, Kathryn "Sis" Bernheim (Fine), Helen McGilvery, Nancy Batson (Crews), and Gertrude Meserve (Tubbs) study the P-39 Airacobra specifications at the Bell factory in Buffalo, New York, in early 1943 before ferrying the P-39s to California. The P-39 was a single-seater, so there were no checkout rides with an experienced P-39 pilot. (Courtesy of Nancy Crews.)

Four WAFS pilots ferrying aircraft through Craig Field in Selma, Alabama, from left to right, are: B.J. Erickson (London), Barbara Donahue, Ester Manning, and Barbara Poole (Shoemaker). (Courtesy of B.J. Erickson London.)

Woodlawn High School Alumni sold enough war bonds in WW II to buy a Consolidated B-24 Liberator, appropriately named "Woodlawn High." (SMF Photo.)

Five

COLD WARBIRDS,
PRIVATE PROPS, AND
THE PHANTOM

Hayes Aircraft employees gather in front of the first B-25 Mitchell Bomber delivered to Hayes for overhaul during the Korean War. More B-25s were built in WW II than any other twin-engine bombers—9,816. (SMF photo.)

The first two Air Guard P-51 pilots in this photograph are unknown. Left to right from Al Baker in the center are Sam McClurkin and Joe Wilson. (SMF photo.)

The North American P-51 Mustang was the premier long-range escort fighter of WW II, and 15,586 were built. (SMF photo.)

Paul Norman, Joe Shannon, Max Campbell, and Bill Anderson stand between the twin engines of the B-26 Douglas Invader. (SMF photo.)

The B-26 Douglas Invader was the CIA's bomber of choice for the Bay of Pigs because the Cuban Air Force had B-26s, and the CIA cover story was that the Cuban Air Force had joined the invasion to overthrow Castro. The Invader above had as much trouble with its landing gears as the Bay of Pigs invaders had getting support. The mains wouldn't come down and the nose wheel wouldn't go up! (SMF photo.)

Mark Henley in the North American P-51 Mustang often flies in area airshows, including the Birmingham Aero Club's annual fall show at Bessemer Airport. (Courtesy of Mark Henley.)

Richard Woodruff and Austin Landry stand with Richard's North American T-28 Trojan, a two-seater USAF trainer first used in 1949. The T-28's name is "Miss Ann" for Richard's wife, Ann Woodruff. (Courtesy of Austin Landry.)

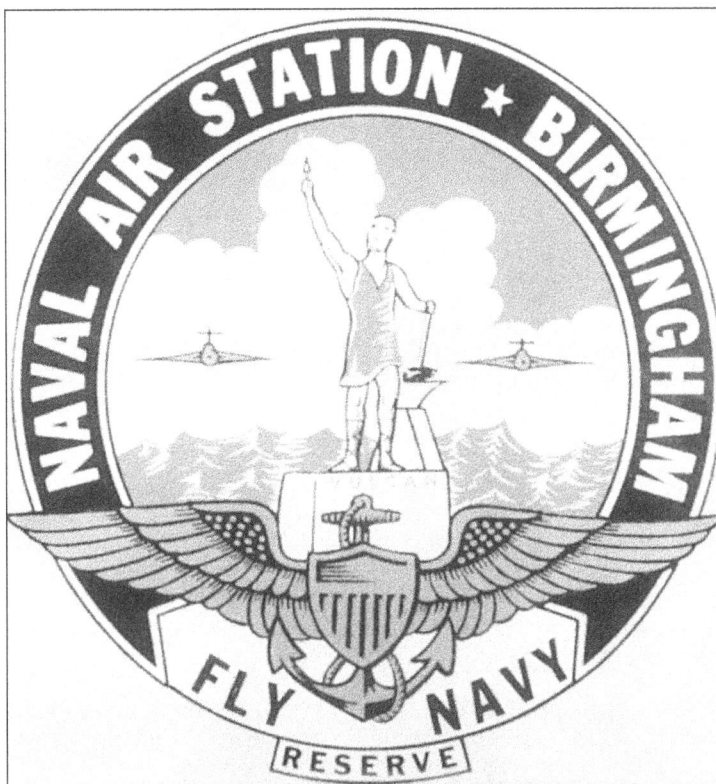

Commander R.F. Lewellyn (far right), Naval Air Station (NAS) Atlanta, reads commissioning orders of NARDIV 671, Birmingham, to the following men, pictured from left to right, Commander J.M. Weaver, Officer-in-Charge, Navy/Marine Training Center; Lt. Commander Luther J. Strange, Commanding Officer NARDIV 671; and Chief W.D. McGinty, Administrator of NARDIV. (SMF photo.)

The Vought Corsair F4U is well known to the general public through the television series *Baa Baa Black Sheep*. Longtime museum supporter Ralph Zorn flew the Corsair in WW II, and Zorn's plane numbers are on a mural in the BAC meeting room. (SMF photo.)

These NAS Birmingham aircraft, AD-1 "Skyraider" and F8F "Bearcat," have their wings folded for space saving as they would on a carrier. (SMF photo.)

One of NAS Birmingham's patrol planes, the PBY-5S "Catalina," prepares for takeoff. (SMF photo.)

A portion of NAS Birmingham's flight line includes a SNJ trainer (closest aircraft to the photographer), the Navy version of the Museum's AT-6 Texan. The Hayes Corporation B-29 modification center is in the background. (SMF photo.)

Hayes Aircraft Corporation at the Birmingham Municipal Airport was a major Birmingham employer after WW II. Its role in repairing aircraft was performed by Bechtel-McCone earlier and PEMCO currently. (SMF photo.)

Lou Jeffers, on the extreme left, hosts Dr. Wernher von Braun's 1958 tour of Hayes Aircraft. (SMF photo.)

A pensive Joe Shannon scans Bay of Pigs literature in the SMF store. Note the 1961 photo of Lt. Col. Shannon highlighted by the U.S. flags. (SMF photo.)

Seen here is the B-26 Douglas Invader flown by Alabama Air National Guardsman Joe Shannon, Operations Officer, in the Bay of Pigs invasion. (Courtesy of Joe Shannon.)

Guardsman Riley Shamburger's B-26 Douglas Invader was shot down by a Cuban T-33 and crashed into the sea. Shamburger was the Assistant Operation Officer for the training of the Cuban pilots. Joe Shannon narrowly escaped being shot down by the same T-33. (SMF photo.)

Guardsman Leo Baker was shot down and killed in the Bay of Pigs invasion in April 1961. Sixteen Americans flew support missions for the Cuban Liberation Army and four were killed. The museum does not have a photo of Wade Gray. Leo Baker's CIA medal is in the Bay of Pigs case at the SMF. (SMF photo.)

Guardsman Pete Ray was shot down in the latter stage of the Bay of Pigs invasion. He survived the crash, but was shot and killed at close range by Cuban infantrymen. After years of effort by his daughter, Janet, his body was finally returned to the United States. (SMF photo.)

Norm Ponder (on the left) watches the "Navy guys from Fallon" reassemble the T-33 jet trainer for the Bay of Pigs exhibit. Mike Callahan operates the 5-ton crane. (SMF photo.)

John Burgin is checking the cockpit of the Museum's B-26 Douglas Invader to determine restoration needs for the Bay of Pigs exhibit. (SMF photo.)

Lynn Sumner Jared and husband Mike Jared (top center) with their parents, Mr. and Mrs. Alan Jared (left) and Mr. and Mrs. Thurston Sumner (right), survey a navigation chart on the tail of the Jared's Cessna 182 four-seater. With Sumner's Beechcraft Bonanza six-seater, the Jareds and Sumners once took trips together as far away as Central America and the Bahamas. (Courtesy of Mike and Lynn Jared.)

Richard Reeve is pictured with his Beechcraft Bonanza A36. (Courtesy of Richard Reeve.)

Dr. Ed Stevenson is shown in his Pitts S-1 Special (above) and Citabria (below). In recent years, Stevenson flew to more than 30 airports delivering materials for the Southern Museum of Flight. (Courtesy of Ed Stevenson.)

Richard Simpson's Fleet 16B-NC41DJ is pictured here. (Courtesy of Richard Simpson.)

Richard Simpson is seen with his E-2 Cub-NC 2122. The E-2 was the first Cub manufactured by Taylor-Piper Aircraft. The next model was the J-2 Cub which he and John Burgin are now restoring at the museum. (Courtesy of Richard Simpson.)

Nancy Crews has a Piper J-3 Cub, the first Cub that was mass-produced. (Courtesy of Nancy Crews.)

Opal Kindberg soloed in a Cherokee 140 in 1969 and promptly joined the Civil Air Patrol. She has flown search-and-rescue missions for 25 years and served as CO, Squadron 34, CAP for ten years. She owned a Cessna 182 but currently flies a Cessna 172. (Courtesy of Opal Kindberg.)

An Alabama National Guard F-4 Phantom flies over the Air Guard hangars at Birmingham International Airport. (SMF Photo.)

Pictured are Mayor Richard Arrington (mayor 1979–1999) and Colonel Cecil Greene (F-4 pilot and later major general) at the National Veterans Day dinner, November 11, 1989. (Courtesy Cecil Greene.)

Colonel Pewitt's WSO "gib" (guy in back), crew chief, and Colonel Pewitt are pictured in Vietnam in 1972 after Pewitt's 100th mission. (Courtesy of J. Dudley Pewitt.)

Dr. J. Dudley Pewitt is seen in front of an F-4 Phantom with his Vietnam numbers, complimenting the mural painter and former Russian MiG-21 pilot Serguei Timtchenko. (SMF photo.)

Colonel Cecil Greene welcomes Maj. Gen. Colin Powell back to Birmingham in the early 1980s. General Powell's wife, Alma, is the daughter of Robert Johnson, former principal of Parker High School. (Courtesy of Cecil Greene.)

Mayor Richard Arrington welcomes Secretary of Defense Caspar Weinburger to Birmingham. Weinburger was the guest of honor for the 37th annual Veterans Day celebration (1983) and spoke at the World Peace Luncheon at Boutwell Auditorium. (Courtesy of Cecil Greene.)

The museum's F-4 Phantom turns off 73rd Street north at 43rd Avenue as it is maneuvered into place in front of the museum. Through the assistance of Mayor Arrington, the Southern Museum of Flight became the first civilian aviation museum to have an F-4. (Courtesy of Cecil Greene.)

Alabama Air Guardsmen gather around their central aircraft of recent decades—the McDonnell Douglas F-4 Phantom. (SMF photo.)

Pictured is the rear of the F-4 Phantom in front of the Southern Museum of Flight. (Courtesy of Bob Kendrick.)